Blue
A secret
agent

**Chief
Stella Bird**
The boss

Perch
Stella Bird's
assistant

Professor Z
Invents
gadgets

**Astronaut
Wing**
Flies
Falcon 8

**Commander
Beak**
Runs the Pigeon
Space Station

Written by
Debbie White

Illustrated by
Rebecca Clements

The Baddies

Birdseed

Villain that wants
to be famous

Robo-Dove

Birdseed's
giant robot

WAL

D1102408

904 000 00496937

OXFORD

UNIVERSITY PRESS

Great Clarendon Street, Oxford, OX2 6DP, United Kingdom

Oxford University Press is a department of the University of Oxford.
It furthers the University's objective of excellence in research, scholarship,
and education by publishing worldwide. Oxford is a registered trade mark
of Oxford University Press in the UK and in certain other countries

Text © Debbie White 2015
Illustrations © Oxford University Press 2015

The moral rights of the author have been asserted

First published 2015

British Library Cataloguing in Publication Data
Data available

ISBN: 978-0-19-835680-6

10 9 8 7 6 5 4 3 2

Paper used in the production of this book is a natural, recyclable product
made from wood grown in sustainable forests. The manufacturing process
conforms to the environmental regulations of the country of origin.

Printed in China by Leo Paper Products Ltd

Acknowledgements

Series Advisor: Nikki Gamble
Illustrated by Rebecca Clements
Designed by Oxford University Press in collaboration with Miranda Costa

2

4

There are satellites in space, above Earth. Signals from satellites help people to watch TV and make phone calls.

Satellites in action

A TV show from here ...

1

... is sent to TVs here ...

... here ...

... and here.

3

A boy in Singapore phones ...

... his Dad in Australia.

At the Pigeon Spy Agency, Chief Stella Bird isn't happy.

How many satellites are there above Earth, Agent Blue?

Thousands, Chief!

Well, all the TV satellites have disappeared. No more *Pop Pigeons* until we get them back.

Oh no!

You need to go to the Pigeon Space Station to find out what's going on … I suspect Birdseed is causing trouble again!

First, Blue tries scuba diving to get an idea of what it feels like to float in space.

Ever been scuba diving before, Blue?

No, Sir!

Next, Blue experiences what take-off will feel like.

Feeling a bit sick, Sir ...

Don't mess up your spacesuit!

Professor Z and Astronaut Wing show Blue the controls on *Falcon 8*.

Press the Wallaby Warp Drive button to travel super-fast.

Why is it called that?

You travel super-fast but you bounce like a wallaby.

BOING BOING

Can you guess what the Hedgehog Defence Shield does?

Does it make *Falcon 8* all prickly?

Correct! And the Chameleon Cloaking Device makes *Falcon 8* look like ANYTHING you want!

Wing takes Blue to a special training room.

I'm going to show you how to do things while you are weightless.

WEIGHTLESS

First they practise eating while weightless ...

I've never had to chase my beans before!

... then sleeping ...

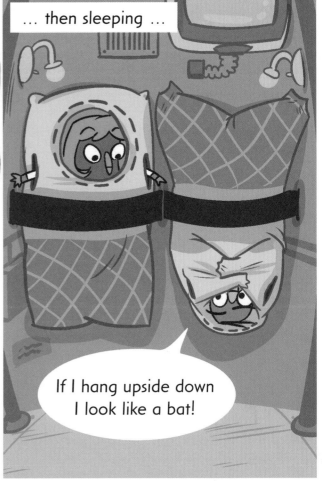

If I hang upside down I look like a bat!

The next day, Blue and Wing wait for blast-off. Chief calls Blue on the video-phone.

Good luck, Agent Blue. Remember, we need those satellites back!

Yes, Chief!

BLAST-OFF!

10 9 8 7 6 5 4 3 2 1

Blue's stomach flips. The force pins him to his seat and he can't move a feather.

The rocket and shuttle separate.

Coo ... I'm in space!

Wing points out of the shuttle window.

Look!

The Pigeon Space Station! Hooray!

Yes, but what's that shadow behind it?

As they get closer, they can see the name 'Swirly Whirly' on the side of the strange shape.

SWIRLY WHIRLY

The Swirly Whirly thing is getting very close to the Pigeon Space Station …

I don't like it, Wing. We have to stop it!

But it's too late. The Space Station is sucked into the Swirly Whirly.

THUNK!

Blue and Wing gasp in horror. Suddenly, a familiar voice booms out over the video-phone …

Who's a clever pigeon, then?

BIRDSEED!

We meet again, Agent Blue. Do you like my Swirly Whirly?

What IS that thing?

It's a remote-controlled super vacuum that sucks up anything that gets in its way!

16

Swirly Whirly heads off into space looking for more satellites.

If we don't get there soon, we're going to run out of fuel!

How soon?

We've got around 20 minutes of flying time left!

Coo ... OK, this is the plan ...

A minute later, Wing flies *Falcon 8* close to the mouth of Swirly Whirly.

I hope this works, Blue.

So do I. It's going to need split-second timing.

Falcon 8 gets sucked inside the Swirly Whirly.

Engage the Hedgehog Defence Shield. Now!

SALURP!

EEH! OOH! AAH!

THUNK!

HICCUP!

The hedgehog spikes stick into the sides of Swirly Whirly.
Has the plan worked?

Swirly Whirly detects the blockage.
It engages its reverse suction.

BLOCKAGE DETECTED.

REVERSE SUCTION.

What does 'reverse suction' mean?

Hold on, Wing. I think we're about to find out!

Blue and Wing have everything crossed.

Swirly Whirly's reverse suction tries to blow Falcon 8 back out into space. It is super-powerful!

Let's hope the hedgehog spikes hold us in place!

Two hours later ... Swirly Whirly, with *Falcon 8* still stuck inside, reaches Birdseed's Space Base.

We're stopping, Blue. What do we do next?

Swirly Whirly lands. Wing turns off the Hedgehog Defence Shield and sets the Chameleon Cloaking Device to 'invisible'.

Blue and Wing jump out of *Falcon 8*. They creep through Swirly Whirly and into Birdseed's Space Base.

Wow! It's HUGE!

You stay here with *Falcon 8*, while I search for Birdseed.

But what if Blue doesn't come back? I'm going to follow him.

Blue isn't sure which way to go. But someone has been eating popcorn ... and they've been dropping bits.

Yum! I'll follow the popcorn trail. It must lead somewhere.

Mmm ... yum.

What's this up ahead?

Suddenly, Blue finds himself in a huge control room. He quickly hides but it's too late.

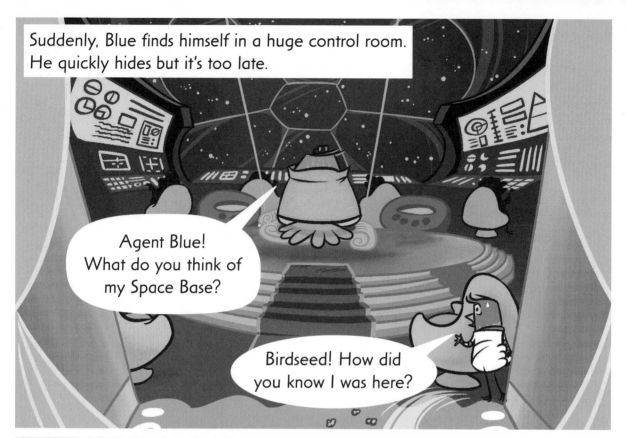

Robo-Dove's eyes light up and she charges at Blue.

Eeek!

Blue turns and flies away but Robo-Dove is fast. Her beak snaps at Blue's tail.

You can fly, Blue, but you can't hide.

Robo-Dove chases Blue around Birdseed's Space Base.
Just as Blue is about to lose his tail feathers ...

... someone grabs him and
pulls him into a cupboard.

Wing! What are you
doing here?

Saving you from
Robo-Dove!

Thanks, Wing. We can't stay in this cupboard forever though. How will we get past Robo-Dove?

Even in the dark cupboard, Blue can see that Wing is smiling.

Birdseed STOLE Robo-Dove …

Who from?

The Pigeon Space Station!

So …?

On the count of three, they burst out of the cupboard.

Blue distracts Robo-Dove with some interesting dance moves ...

Like my funky chicken dance, Robo-Dove?

What about ballet? Do you know *Swan Lake*?

Whoop, whoop ... Birdman-style!

... while Wing plucks a feather from her wing.

Robo-Dove is so distracted, she doesn't even notice when Wing flies under her arm.

Tickle, tickle!

Robo-Dove falls to the floor, laughing.

Hee! Hee!

Quickly, Blue reaches under Robo-Dove's wing and presses the button.

CLICK WHIRRR PING!

Birdseed's the enemy. Blue is your friend.

Robo-Dove turns to Blue, smiling.

Horrible Birdseed. Best friend Blue.

Coo … it worked, Wing! But we still need to stop Birdseed.

You think you can stop me, Agent Blue?

Blast! Birdseed's snuck up on us.

Robo-Dove, grab them and bring them to me!

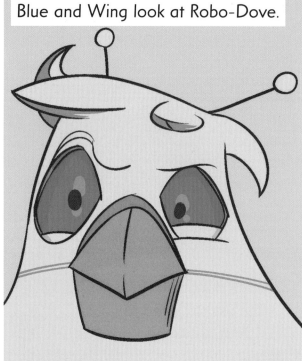

Blue and Wing look at Robo-Dove.

Uh oh. Something's wrong. Robo-Dove should be scaring Blue ... but she's scaring ME!

Big hug, Birdseed.

Birdseed can see the glint in Robo-Dove's eyes. She is planning to give him a VERY big hug indeed.

Argh ... I'm off! But don't get too comfortable, Agent Blue. I'll be back!

Birdseed runs away. Robo-Dove, Blue and Wing race after him.

They are too slow. Birdseed flies away in his escape pod ... Robo-Dove chases after him.

Birdseed's getting away again!

Never mind. We have his Space Base and Swirly Whirly. We can catch him later.

WHOOMP
WHOOMP
WHOOMP

We need a plan to get the satellites back and working again.

We might even be home in time to watch *Pop Pigeons*!

Robo-Dove shows Blue and Wing how to operate the remote controls for Swirly Whirly. They fly Swirly Whirly back out into space and press the Reverse Suction button.

BVVVVVVVVVVV

Look! There's the Pigeon Space Station! Call them to check they're OK.

Agent Blue to Pigeon Space Station ... come in Space Station.

CRACKLE...! fizzzz... CRACKLE...

A few nervous seconds later ...

This is Commander Beak at the Pigeon Space Station. Who am I talking to?

This is Astronaut Wing and Agent Blue. Are you all OK?

We're fine. Thank you for rescuing us. It was very dark and dusty in there!

Good to see you've rescued Robo-Dove, too!

Chirp!

One hour later ... Commander Beak arrives and takes control of Birdseed's Space Base and Swirly Whirly.

There will be no more mischief from Birdseed while I'm in charge!

Good to hear it, sir. What about Robo-Dove? Will she go back to the Pigeon Space Station?

I think she's earned herself a holiday first. Why don't you take her back to Earth with you on *Falcon 8*?

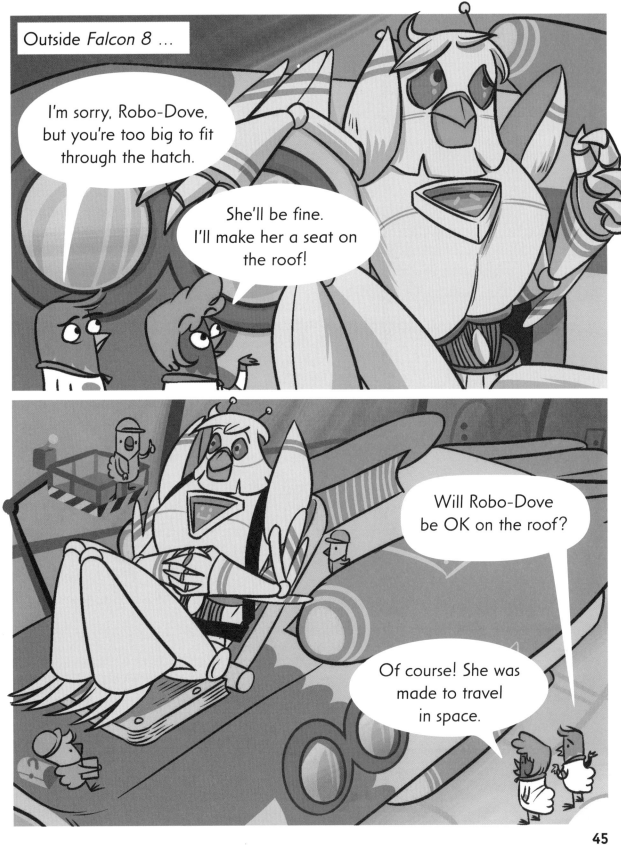

OK, Wing. Let's head home!

Robo-Dove has a brilliant time. It's like bouncing around on a giant trampoline!

Chief Stella Bird, Perch and Professor Z are waiting when they land.

Well done, Blue and Wing! All the satellites are working again … and I'm pleased to see you've brought … er …

Robo-Dove, Chief. Birdseed stole her from the Pigeon Space Station. Commander Beak said she could come to Earth for a holiday.

Aah ... THAT Robo-Dove. Excellent!

To celebrate their safe return, Chief invites everyone to her house to have tea and watch *Pop Pigeons*.